The Story of
CONFUCIUS II

www.royalcollins.com

*Picture Story Book of
Ancient Chinese Thinkers*

The Story of
CONFUCIUS II

Guo Defu

Translated by Wu Meilian

Picture Story Books of Ancient Chinese Thinkers
The Story of CONFUCIUS II

Guo Defu
Translated by Wu Meilian

First published in 2024 by Royal Collins Publishing Group Inc.
Groupe Publication Royal Collins Inc.
550-555 boul. René-Lévesque O Montréal (Québec) H2Z1B1 Canada

Copyright © Jinan Publishing House Co., Ltd.
This English edition is authorized by Jinan Publishing House Co., Ltd.

All rights reserved. Without limiting the rights under copyright reserved above, no part of this publication may be reproduced, stored in or introduced into a retrieval system, or transmitted in any form or by any means (electronic, mechanical, photocopying, recording, or otherwise), without the prior written permission of both the copyright owner and the above publisher of this book.

ISBN: 979-8-9852490-3-3

To find out more about our publications, please visit www.royalcollins.com.

Duke Jing of Qi met with Confucius and asked him how to govern a country. Confucius answered, "The most important thing about governing a country is to be frugal."

His disciples asked him why, and he said, "Duke Jing of Qi builds luxurious houses and gardens, he has court singers and dancers perform for him without stop, and he has awarded his officials rich fiefs with thousands of war carriages three times in one morning. That is why I gave him this advice."

In addition to the Shao Music, Confucius also watched *taju* (also called *cuju*)* in Linzi.

---

* *Cuju* was a sport similar to today's football. During the Spring and Autumn Period (770–476 BCE), *cuju* was used to train and examine soldiers' physiques.

Cuju games were often held whenever there were grand events or celebrations, and many of Confucius's friends and disciples from Qi were *cuju* lovers.

With the help of Qi minister Gao Zhaozi, Confucius was received by Duke Jing. The duke decided to appoint Confucius to a high position and grant him a fief after several in-depth conversations. However, the Qi ministers were opposed to such an idea, and some even tried to murder Confucius to prevent him from gaining benefits in Qi.

When they learned about the danger they were in, Confucius and his disciples were just starting to cook. Confucius thus took the uncooked rice out of the pot, and when they quickly took off from the lodging, the wet rice was still dripping water from his hands.

On his way from the State of Qi to the State of Lu, Confucius passed Mount Tai. He climbed the dangerous mountain to see the sunrise. The spectacular scene filled Confucius's heart with love for the world.

Confucius's disciple, Gongye Chang, was an upright, hardworking student. Once, he was wronged and put in jail. Confucius said to him, "I know you are innocent," and insisted that Gongye be his son-in-law. The young couple had a happy life together and had two sons, Zili and Zigeng.

Gongye Chang devoted his life to learning and teaching, and he later became a renowned scholar. He had planted two ginkgo trees with his wife and his master in his former residence in Anqiu, Shandong Province, and they can still be seen today.

Confucius valued his family highly. His half-brother Mengpi suffered from a congenital foot disease, so Confucius often returned to his hometown to visit and accompany his older brother.

He became the teacher of his nephew Kong Zhong (courtesy name Zimie) and taught him to become honest and erudite. He also introduced his outstanding disciple, Nangong Kuo, to marry his niece. After Mengpi died, Confucius buried him next to their parents' graves.

Confucius put great emphasis on his son's education. In addition to letting his son Kong Li attend his lessons with other disciples, he paid a lot of attention to his choices and progress in learning. In *The Analects*, Confucius taught his son, "If you do not learn the Odes, you will not be fit to converse with. If you do not learn the rules of Propriety, your character cannot be established."

His academic and life teachings deeply influenced his son Kong Li and his grandson Zisi and prepared them to become excellent scholars as well.

Based on the physiological conditions at different stages of human lives, Confucius proposed the "Three Precepts for Health Preservation" and "Phase Prescription for Health Preservation." He emphasized that different health rules should be followed at different periods. In teenage years, one's physiological structure is still developing, and one should refrain from indulging in lust to ensure normal development of health; in the prime of life, one's vitality and body are fully developed, and one should thus refrain from anger and aggressiveness; in old age, attention should be paid to health maintenance, and one should refrain from greed and having too much desire.

Confucius asked his disciples to talk about their aspirations when they traveled to Mount Nong. Zilu said loudly, "I wish to go to the battlefield for my country when she is at war and fight back against all enemies by myself." Confucius answered, "You are a brave warrior!"

Zigong said, "I wish to solve crises between countries at war by persuading the kings to retreat."

Confucius answered, "You are an eloquent speaker."

Yan Hui said, "I wish to assist a wise king, carry out benevolent ruling, and eliminate the possibility of wars." Confucius praised him.

When a blind musician visited Confucius, the latter welcomed him in person, assisted him to his seat, and informed him of everyone as well as their locations in the room. After the musician left, disciple Zizhang asked, "Master, should we all treat blind people the way you did today?"

Confucius replied, "This is the most basic courtesy to address blind people."

When Confucius fished, he never used a fishing net with multiple hooks. He set a good example for people today in protecting nature while utilizing natural resources. In Shandong Province, we can still see the site where Confucius used to fish.

Confucius was a skilled archer, but he never shot birds that were resting in their nests, thinking of the fledglings that needed their parents. He was practicing the very modern concept of sustainable development even 2,500 years ago.

Yang Huo, Lu Minister Ji Huanzi's retainer, was now in power in the State of Lu and wished to have Confucius serve him. He first spread the word to urge the meeting, but Confucius pretended not to know and did not come. Then, Yang Huo sent a steamed suckling pig as a present to Confucius' when he was not at home, leaving Confucius no choice but to visit him according to the Zhou rituals.

Knowing Yang Huo's intention, Confucius tried to avoid him and returned the favor when he was not at home. However, he ran into Yang Huo on his way back. Yang Huo asked Confucius to serve him in court, but Confucius did not comply. Sometime later, Yang Huo was defeated in a coup, thus ending his regime.

At fifty-one, Confucius was appointed governor of Zhongdu by Duke Ding of Lu. After Confucius took office, he formulated a series of policies to benefit the people, and in just one year, the people of Zhongdu were able to live and work in peace and contentment.

Soon, Confucius was promoted. People came to see him off and presented him with countless local products, but Confucius declined them all.

The only thing he accepted was a pair of new fabric shoes made by an old man who wished to replace them with Confucius' old shoes as a souvenir. Confucius set off wearing the new shoes, feeling warm and fulfilled.

Confucius was promoted to the Grand Judge of the State of Lu, in charge of public security and justice.

At that time, counterfeiting was common in Qufu. A sheep dealer named Chenyou gave the sheep a lot of water early in the morning and then sold them at higher prices. Other livestock dealers would sell shoddy products as good ones and try whatever means to raise the price.

After taking office, Confucius decided to change the situation with moral teaching and legal punishment, and his methods soon achieved remarkable results. Chenyou no longer sold watered sheep, the livestock dealers no longer sold shoddy goods, and some dishonest merchants fled the State of Lu. The whole society became harmonious.

After Confucius was promoted to the Grand Judge of Lu, he declined the fine chariot and horses assigned to him by the duke and only used simple wooden carriages and ordinary horses.

He set an example for the Lu officials to be frugal and changed the luxurious style in the State of Lu.

In the summer of 500 BCE, the States of Qi and Lu met in Jiagu (now Laiwu, Shandong Province) to form an alliance. During the meeting, the Qi people tried to kidnap the Duke of Lu during a sword dance.

At the critical moment, Confucius, Lu's chief military officer, risked his life and loudly rebuked the Qi people for being disrespectful with justice and etiquette, thus safeguarding the dignity and interests of his country.

In order to achieve national stability and unity, Confucius suggested "abandoning the three capitals" of Fei, Hou, and Cheng established by the Jisun, Shusun, and Mengsun families, thereby weakening the power of the "Three Huan."*

---

* The "Three Huan" refers to the Jisun, Shusun, and Mengsun families in the State of Lu. Since the three families were all descendants of Duke Huan of Lu, they were called the "Three Huan."

During the implementation, Gongshan Buniu from Fei started a rebellion, which was put down by Confucius. However, he encountered strong opposition from the Mengsun family when demolishing the city walls. As the dissatisfaction of the "Three Huan" against him increased, Confucius fell into trouble in Lu's political arena.

Confucius' assistantship made the State of Lu increasingly powerful, and the monarchs and ministers of the State of Qi felt threatened. They came up with a plan and gave Duke Ding of Lu many beautiful women and good horses, which led to Duke Ding and his minister Ji Huanzi abandoning political affairs. After the State Sacrifice Ceremony, Ji Huanzi did not distribute the sacrificial meat to Confucius as usual. This meant that Confucius was isolated from Lu's political arena. He and his disciples thus decided to find a way out in another state.

At Tundi, Confucius and his party met Shi Ji, who was sent by Ji Huanzi to see him off. Confucius was disappointed to know that the court had no intention of keeping him. Before leaving, he said: "Let's walk slowly. This is how we leave our home country." The 55-year-old Confucius left the State of Lu and began a long journey traveling around the other states.

Confucius' party traveled west to the State of Wei, but the Duke Ling of Wei did not pay much attention to them.

One day, Wangsun Jia, a powerful minister of Wei, came to Confucius and said: "It's better to worship the kitchen god than the home god." Although the home god had a more noble status, the kitchen god had more control over the homeowner's luck. So, many people at that time liked to give more offerings to the kitchen god, hoping he could report good things about the family and bring back good luck from Heaven.

Wangsun Jia's intention was obvious: he could help with Confucius' employment in the Wei court, but Confucius would need to give him some benefits. Confucius refused and said, "One has nothing to pray for if he offends Heaven." A person must be honest and upright if he wishes help from Heaven.

Duke Ling of Wei's wife Nanzi was very beautiful. She was from the State of Song and liked rituals and ceremonial music very much. She knew about Confucius and his story of exploring the rites and music of Song when he was young and marrying a Song woman. Now, hearing that he was in the State of Wei, she would very much like to meet with him.

She said, "I will meet with anyone who comes to Wei to be brothers with the king," and Confucius received her invitation. After returning, he said to his students: "I did not meet with her out of my own will, but I found that she understood rites and music quite well after our meeting."

Legend has it that when Shun succeeded to the position of leader of the tribal alliance, he led the people to worship Heaven and Earth and chant the poem "South Wind." Later generations regarded this day as the beginning of the year and thus began the tradition of the Spring Festival.

The "South Wind" expresses the peaceful emotions of nourishing and loving people and has been highly praised by all dynasties. Confucius loved to sing this poem at the Spring Festival and put up a pile of jujube steamed buns according to his hometown's tradition. He commented on the poem as a "flowing stream of virtue not forgotten by lords and ministers till this day."

When Confucius was passing through a village in Xun County in the State of Wei, the cow pulling their cart was about to give birth. Neither Confucius nor his disciples knew what to do. The villagers invited them to their homes and helped take care of the cow until it successfully gave birth to a calf. Confucius taught the *Book of Songs* to the villagers to thank them for their help.

Before he left, he gave the calf to the villagers, who then changed the name of their village to *liuniu* (the cow left behind) to commemorate Confucius.

Confucius only lived in Wei for ten months before he was forced to leave and planned to go to the State of Jin. On their way, Confucius said to the students, "I don't know what a person without integrity can do. How can a cart without the bolt connecting the shaft and yoke move?"

Confucius and his students traveled from one state to another, looking for opportunities to realize their ideals and teaching along their way. Once, on their way to the State of Song, they stopped and set up a temporary school under a big tree.

Huan Tui, the military administrator of the State of Song, was resentful of Confucius because the latter once criticized him for wasting manpower and material resources on building a stone coffin for three years. He sent people to cut down the big tree and threatened to kill Confucius. Confucius and his students had no choice but to flee to the State of Zheng.

The party was separated on their way. Confucius stood alone at the east gate, worried and depressed. At the same time, Zigong was looking anxiously for his master when a passerby told him, "There is a man standing at the east gate, wretched as a stray dog."

After Zigong found Confucius, he told his master what he had heard. "True! True!" he laughed.

Before his death, Ji Huanzi asked his son Ji Kangzi to call Confucius back to Lu. However, due to official Gongzhi Yu's obstruction, Ji Kangzi did not send for Confucius but for his student Ran Qiu.

Before Ran Qiu left, Confucius said to him, "The State of Lu has big plans for you. Go back; you are a man with great ambitions!"

In 489 BCE, Confucius and his students set off for the State of Chu. The kings of Chen and Cai were worried that this would be disadvantageous to them, so they sent people to besiege Confucius's party between the two states.

For seven days, Confucius and his students had no food, and they were starving and became sick. Nevertheless, Confucius remained calm, and he continued to give lectures, recite poems, and play music to the students. Seven days later, they were finally out of trouble.

Once, Confucius and his students came to a river but couldn't find the ferry, so Zilu went to seek help from two people working in the fields nearby. He first went to Changju, who replied, "If your master really is Confucius, then he should know the way."

Zilu then went to Jieni, who replied, "This chaotic, declining world is like a torrential flood; who has the ability to change it? Aren't you teachers and students also living in exile and running into obstacles everywhere? Why not make a living by farming like us?"

Confucius looked up to the sky and sighed, "Don't I want to live undisturbed in the mountains and forests? But someone has to make sacrifices to make the world a better place!" Thus came the idiom "finding the lost ferry," which shows Confucius' indomitable spirit of saving the world.

Confucius' journey across the States of Wei, Cao, Chen, and Chu did not help him realize his ultimate political ideals, but the hardships perfected his virtues and enriched his knowledge.

By the campfires during the trips, when the corn porridge was cooking, he dreamed of the golden phoenix, symbolizing peace and prosperity, spreading its wings and bringing a benevolent government to the world where everyone is allowed access to education, where people live in peace and trust.

During his travels, Confucius learned that Qi's army was going to invade Lu, so he hurriedly sent Zigong to lobby the leaders of the other states to buy time for Lu to prepare for the war. He also sent a brief letter to Ran Qiu and Fan Chi in Lu, who then trained a commando team with long spears according to the techniques their master had taught them.

With this team, Ran Qiu led the Lu army and defeated Qi. After the great victory, someone asked Ran Qiu where he had learned such skills, and Ran Qiu replied, "From my master Confucius."

In the face of the crisis, Ran Qiu and Fan Chi did not flinch. When the Lu army was in danger, Fan Chi loudly encouraged the soldiers to defend their state and stepped forward to be the first to attack; Ran Qiu used his spear to defeat the enemy.

When Confucius heard this, he said happily, "What righteous men they are!"

In 484 BCE, Ji Kangzi finally sent people to welcome Confucius back to the State of Lu, and Confucius' 14 years of traveling life ended at the age of 68.

On his way home, Confucius passed by a valley and saw an orchid growing among the weeds. Fascinated by the flower's elegance and beauty, Confucius stopped and sang, "The mountain breeze is blowing, rain is coming behind the clouds. Now, you are returning to a faraway land, and we see you off in the wild. Why is there no place for you under heaven? Why can't you find anywhere to stay in the world? The world knows no worthy man. As time goes by, I will grow old."

After returning to the State of Lu, Confucius concentrated on studying and teaching. The Xizou Village in Qufu, where Confucius revised the *Spring and Autumn Annals* and compiled ancient texts, also became well-known for the *Song of Xizou* that he composed. The *Spring and Autumn Annals* was the first chronicle-style history book in China. It records the 242-year history of the Spring and Autumn Period (244 years according to *The Commentary of Zuo*) and covers the various aspects of contemporary politics, military, economy, culture, astronomy, meteorology, material production, and social life.

The *Spring and Autumn Annals* originally served as a textbook for Confucius' students. It was written with concise language with implicit praise and criticism of historical events. In his own words, "People can understand me through the *Spring and Autumn Annals*, and people can criticize me about the *Spring and Autumn Annals*!"

Confucius loved to sing and play instruments. He composed songs and had a profound understanding of music. He said, "Music is understandable. When it starts to play, the notes appear one after another, lively and enthusiastic; then, the sounds are simple and harmonious, the rhythm is clear and bright, and the melody continues until the end of the song." Confucius used to play the flute in Queli, he sang in the States of Chen and Cai, and he played the chimes in the capital of Wei. He considered music as "the harmony of the heaven and earth!"

After Confucius returned to the State of Lu, he composed music for the more than 300 poems in the *Book of Songs* so that "the hymns and the eulogies are all in place."

One of his students, Zixia, continued to help Confucius with the compilation until his later years. After Confucius had finished his work with the *Book of Songs*, he taught it all to Zixia.

Confucius advocated that poetry and music could not be separated. He used poems with music to express his aspirations and to communicate with others through singing. The integration of poetry, music, and etiquette created the Confucian education system that "starts with poetry, is established with etiquette, and is completed with music."

When Confucius finally returned home, his wife, Qiguan, had already passed away. But soon, the birth of his grandson Kong Ji, courtesy name Zisi, relieved the old man's sorrow and brought him new hope for the future.

Little Zisi was very smart, and Confucius' love for him grew after his father, Kong Li, passed away. Confucius took Zisi by his side, and they worked and played together—when Confucius compiled books, Zisi played with the bamboo slips (which were the books of that time).

Zisi grew up day by day and lived up to his grandfather's teachings. He could recite simple verses when he was young and eventually became a famous Confucian scholar. He was the author of *The Doctrine of the Mean*, one of the "Four Books and Five Classics," and he educated many outstanding students, such as Mencius.

Confucius liked planting trees. He and his students planted many trees in front of the apricot altar, and one cypress tree is still vigorous today.

When Confucius went to visit his son-in-law, Gongye Chang, he brought a few saplings as a present. A ginkgo tree he planted with his students in Shangcai County, Henan Province, can still be seen flourishing.

Once, Shen Zhuliang asked Zilu what kind of person his teacher was, but Zilu did not answer. When Confucius heard this, he said, "You may tell him that I often study and forget to eat. When I make discoveries and progress in my knowledge, I get so happy that I forget all my sorrow and even ignore the passing of my life." Confucius achieved the highest state of life by forgetting the world and himself with his lifelong love for learning.

Confucius had a dog. He loved it very much and often took it for walks. When he was lecturing at the apricot altar, the dog would lay quietly by his side as if listening to his lessons. It seemed to have developed a love for books and never trampled on the books that Confucius sometimes put in the courtyard. When the dog died of old age, Confucius was very sad.

He said to Zigong, "Give it a proper burial. I hear that horses are buried with old cart curtains, and dogs are buried with old cart covers. I am poor and don't have old cart covers, so just wrap it up in a mat." Zigong buried the dog beside the Si River, where Confucius often took it for walks.

Confucius organized the vast collection of ancient literature and classics from different states into "Six Classics": the *Book of Songs*, the *Book of Documents*, the *Book of Rites*, the *Classic of Music*, the *Book of Changes*, and the *Spring and Autumn Annals*.

The *Book of Changes* is an ancient Chinese philosophy book, known as *Zhou Yi*, *Yi Jing*, and *Yi*. It is praised as "the top of all scriptures and the source of the great Way."

In his later years, Confucius was very devoted to the *Book of Changes* and studied it repeatedly, even breaking the leather ropes connecting the bamboo slips many times. The idiom "ropes repeatedly break" commemorates this story. Confucius said, "If I could live a few more years, I would fully grasp the essence of the *Book of Changes*."

When he was seventy-one years old, his favorite student, Yan Hui, died at the age of forty-one. Confucius was overwhelmed by grief, and he cried, "Heaven is killing me! Heaven is taking my life away from me!" His other students tried to comfort him, but he said, "Who else should I grieve for if not for him?" He was crying for the loss of an excellent student, an ideal successor, and a loving son. The story of Confucius and Yan Hui continued to be told generation after generation as one of the most classic tales representing Chinese culture.

On April 11, 479 BCE, Confucius passed away at the age of seventy-three. On his deathbed, he cried, "Mount Tai is collapsing! The pillar is breaking! The thinker is leaving!"

Confucius was buried at the bank of the Si River. His disciples compiled his speeches and lectures into a book called *The Analects*, which later became an important classic. In the *Records of the Grand Historian*, Sima Qian praised Confucius as "a mountain to be looked up at and the great Way to be followed."

Over his long teaching career, Confucius taught 3,000 students. The thoughts of this great educator and thinker have left a profound impact on the world for over 2,000 years and will continue to influence the future ages to come.

ABOUT THE AUTHOR

Guo Defu is a famous contemporary Chinese ink-wash painter and representative artist of the Confucian school of painting. With an artistic career of nearly 60 years, he is renowned for his expertise in painting Chinese historical figures. His work, *The Painting Biography of Confucius*, has been exhibited in art exhibitions and book fairs in France, Belgium, Russia, Germany, Australia, Republic of Korea, the United States, and countries along the Belt and Road, allowing audiences from around the world to experience the spirit and charm of Confucius and traditional Chinese culture up close.